Chicago June 2010

Sue-

May peace of mind

be your constant companion-

Shelly

IN THE GARDEN COLLECTION

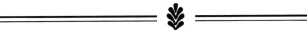

*an inspirational journey
into the heart of the garden*

SHELLY LAWLER

For information, contact Shelly Lawler, shellawler@aol.com

Photos and text by Shelly Lawler

ISBN 978-0-615-33053-2

Published by

Mazzenga Images, LLC

www.mazzengaimages.com

Printed in the United States of America

… to my Val

WELCOME

Each image an invitation

Beckoning

The precious world of the garden...

Peace

DREAM LAND

It's not the days we remember
but the moments...

... moments that lift your spirit
and hold you steady

Comfort you in the promise

Patient,

The Garden waits.

Those who love the garden,

This you know

Arbor Dream

Life meets Light

The Visit

Dawn is my favorite time of day

Full of mystery...

And the limitations have yet to set in.

Morning Light

Morning dew stretching to the sun...

Sparkle

There is a place for you to find...

Rose Garden

A Secret Place

Enchanted

QUIET TIME

Season's Opener...

Spring Time

INVITATION

Melody

Afternoon Tea

Set our table, and make our hearts sing

Iris Sea

Pure Joy

French Bike

Bloom...

Iris

Lily

Out Of The Corner Of My Eye I Saw Something

Oh so fast.

Heard something

Barely

And so,

I would wait for them.

Like a secret filled with sweet anticipation

I would wait for them.

Taking a break from the busyness

in the mid of day

Finches

ROBIN BATH

Misty

Flight

Every moment begins a story...

Romance

Once Upon A Time

LAZY AFTERNOON

WINE & ROSES

AUTUMN DREAM

Yes, I Remember Resting In The Light...

and the warmth of a perfect autumn day.

Safely stored, this memory.

So I can reach and grab and hold it tight.

Feeling hope. Feeling alive.

Once again, resting in the light.

Fall Hat

Waterfall

Sunflower

Night Light

Passage to peace...

Summer Dream

SNOWDROPS

Pecking Order

Trio

THE LIBRARIAN

Far below, yet still above
breathes life in the garden.

Winter Dream

Winter Wonderland

I dreamed of far away places...

Horizon

Of hills and valleys

Tuscany

Of harbors at dawn

At Sea

I dreamed of far away places...

By Candlelight

In The Garden

Wings

PEACE